GOD'S ULTIMATE HEALING POWER

Deliverance Through Her Truth

Keva Pryce

God's Ultimate Healing Power: Deliverance Through Her Truth

Copyright © 2022 by Keva Pryce

Transition Publishing

Missouri City, TX 77489-1361

Unless otherwise indicated, scripture references are from the King James Bible Version

All rights reserved. No part of this book may be reproduced or transmitted in any form or by any means without the written permission from the author.

Table of Content

Preface……………………………………4

Dedication………………………………7

You Are Oh So Beautiful……………8

Chapter 1………………………………11

Chapter 2………………………………18

Chapter 3………………………………40

Chapter 4………………………………49

Chapter 5………………………………65

Keep Me Oh Lord ……………………72

Chapter 6………………………………73

Chapter 7………………………………85

Chapter 8………………………………91

Chapter 9………………………………100

Chapter 10……………………………110

Chapter 11……………………………127

Chapter 12……………………………127

Inter Reflection……………………132

Invitation……………………,,,………135

Preface

This book is about God's ultimate healing power. Here is a story. It may be written in first person or maybe it was told in third person. Maybe I'm reliving a nightmare or maybe I am sharing a friend's testimony. Maybe there are some truths or the whole thing is fabricated, or both may even be mingled in between. Whether this story is true or fictional, it is a story of God's ultimate healing power.

In writing this book I had to travail. That means to "work especially of a painful or laborious nature: toil. A physical or mental exertion or piece of work: task, effort, agony, torment. A woman who is in labor." In writing this book I encountered or revisited much of my own past and history with sexual abuse and turmoil. As a God-fearing woman, youth leader, a minister-in-training and praise dance leader, it is my deepest desire to walk upright as much as I can and be blameless before God. For I know it is written in the Bible that we have all sinned and have fallen short of the glory of God (Romans 3:23), so I can never be perfect, but it is in my striving I can at least attempt. I will be completely honest and transparent in writing this book. My mind has often wandered off in avenues I did not desire for it to go, even my flesh came against me to cause me to want to participate in sexual activities that were ungodly. My motive to be silent about my fleshly desires caused me to run away from writing the book, prolonging the time it should have been done. I knew God was calling me to write the book.

For there is deliverance and healing that needs to take place, but it was my belief that the book was causing me to sin. Because when I would begin to write the book, I felt lustful desires and ungodly temptations rise to the surface. How could a just and righteous God want me to fall to such sin? I found that when I became honest and open when telling my leader/my pastor about the book and what I was writing, the shame that held and hindered me went away.

My pastor gave me vital tools to use as I began writing this book to renounce and rebuke the negative voices. In the bible there is a book called Ruth. The book tells the story of a woman's great tragedy and how she overcomes, however, God's name is never mentioned in the entire book. But you can clearly see Him working in every aspect of her life. It is the same for this book. It is my deepest prayer that even though God's name may not be mentioned in some of the chapters, still you will find Him in between the lines or behind the unspoken words or in the notions of the characters' lives. God is always present even in our darkest hours. Even when we do not speak or mention His name He is there.

Dedication

I dedicate this book to all those who are living in the darkness of being a victim to rape and molestation. I pray God light would expose and begin to heal what is hidden as you begin your journey in this book? The purpose of the light is not to expose you who have been victimized and make you ashamed or embarrassed. Nor is it to make you relive what has been done to you, but it is meant for the exposure to the light to help you begin to heal in His presence. God says in his word. "Luke 8:17, English Standard Version. For nothing is hidden that will not be made manifest, nor is anything secret that will not be known and come to light.

You Are Oh So Beautiful

(By Keva Pryce)

In spite of the scars on your face

They came when you were only eight

Beaten and raped

They put you down making you feel like you had

Yourself to blame

Can't find the courage to run

Thinking you would just go back to square one and I say

You are oh so beautiful

In spite of the lies they told

I heard them say mommy would be mad if you told

So, with tears in your eyes, you tried to hide all the pain

And suffering inside

The secrets you held, hoping, thinking no one would be able to

Tell that this little girl can be going through so much hell

But you are oh so beautiful

From your head to your feet

From what your eyes cannot see

Because you are so unique, and this is not how He wanted it to be

But it had to be

There was no mistake

He predestined and made you to be great

Called you out of darkness

Now you have His grace

Royal priesthood

Favored one

Do not think that He was not there, and He did not care

Because where you are going you had to bear

And I say you are oh so beautiful

Beautiful and make no mistake

Your past is your past

But hold fast, my Lord had a plan for you to pass

And this is why I say, you are oh so beautiful

Beautiful in all your ways that He came down to heal and save, Deliver and now you can rejoice and proclaim

You are oh so beautiful and I make no mistakes

No mistakes in what I say

That what you have been through is not what the Lord has in store for you

And I say you are oh so beautiful

And that is your name.

Chapter 1

Rape - *"unlawful sexual intercourse or any other sexual penetration of the vagina, anus, or mouth of another person, with or without force, by a sex organ, other body part, or foreign object, without the consent of the victim"* - *(dictionary.com).*

It was a Saturday morning. I went over to my best friend's house as normal. He happens to be a boy. It's early in the morning when Stephen opened the door. I entered and immediately learned that his cousin Michael was over for the weekend. Stephen's mom was at work. Michael and I don't get along too well because Michael is fresh and is always trying to feel up on me. Michael is older than my best friend

Stephen, so my friend sometimes didn't come to my rescue. I had to fight him off myself most of the time.

I remember being in the living room watching TV. Michael had called Stephen into his bedroom. Not thinking anything was strange about that, I waited for my friend to return to watch Saturday cartoons with me. But something was strange. I could hear whispering coming from the room they were in and then I heard a countdown 1... 2... 3... Michael and Stephen came running out the room towards me. I jumped up, not sure what was going on. Michael pushed me over the arm of the couch and Stephen grabbed my arms, holding me down. Little did I know I'd been set up and my best friend had betrayed me.

With Stephen holding my arms down and Michael lifting my dress to pull down my underwear, I knew what was about to happen. I was so angry inside but afraid at the same time. I did all I could to fight despite being outnumbered. Using all the strength I had I managed to pull one arm away from Stephen, which allowed me to sucker punch the hell out of Michael. Michael hit the floor from the punch.

Now my so-called best friend had seen me fight in school. I was well-known for wiping ass, so like a coward he ran for his life. As I stepped over Michael to chase after Stephen, Michael grabbed my leg and I hit the floor. Michael got up on me from behind. He grabs my hair, mushing my face into the floor. I couldn't move nor could I release myself from his grasp. Michael managed to get my underwear off, and if I thought his pulling of my hair was painful, the next pain was 100 times worse.

Pulling my legs apart, Michael said, "I got you now." I screamed as the breath left my body. I never felt such pain. Michael yelled for Stephen to come back saying, "I got her! I got her!" I cried with every thrust and push.

Stephen came back and started holding down my arms, but there really was no need since my body was pinned down and I had no fight left in me. It's crazy how two people can be experiencing the same thing and have different reactions. As the tears rolled down my face, I clenched my hands to brace myself for the next thrust against my body. The breathing coming from Michael was so heavy. I could feel his body trembling as he continued to pursue his flesh's gratification.

When Michael finally finished, he then convinced Stephen, who was supposed to be my best friend, to take a turn as if my body was some roller coaster taking them on a thrill ride. In such great disbelief that my so-called best friend would join in such a heinous act.

I was a year older than Stephen. He was always a patsy kind of boy; nevertheless, he was more than just my best friend, he was like a brother to me. We met in kindergarten when some other kids tried to take his afternoon snack. He didn't seem to be the brightest out of the bunch, but I took pity on him anyhow and I beat them up for him. I had been fighting his battles throughout elementary and some of junior high school.

We lived on the same block; his building was just across from mine and our mothers were good friends as well. So, we always hung out. We rode our bikes together sometimes and I would wear my skates and hold on to the back of his bike seat as he rode down the hills. We would play Manhunt with the other kids on the block. I would be the hunter and pretend not to see him so he wouldn't have to be it. Stephen hated to be it because he always had a hard time finding kids. "Stephen, please," I cried out just before he inserted himself into me. "Stop, stop please!" I remember begging to be let go. Michael's hands firmly gripped my arms, pulling them in front of me. Michael asked Stephen, "Now doesn't that feel good?" He encouraged him to keep going and to even push harder as if there were layers to my vagina that felt better than the next. With heavy breathing and stuttering I could hear Stephen respond back to Michael "Yesss."

Time seemed to be eternal, and this ordeal seemed to be endless. Stephen was done a lot faster than Michael. Finally, Michael released me from his grip. In my mind I wanted to quickly take off and run home, but my body would not allow me. Michael and Stephen were standing around me fixing their clothes, waiting to see my next move, but I lay there dormant.

My body ravaged with pain and agony. Fatigue throughout my body.

Somehow, I managed to slowly pull myself from the floor and sit up. Snot and tears were all over my face. I was too afraid to look at Stephen and I was terrified of what Michael would do next. I sat there trying to wrap my dress around my legs. I noticed blood on my legs and between my thighs. There was only silence in the room except for my breathing and whimpering. No words were shared between me and those who had become my violators. I slowly stood to my feet, and I walked out the house. My body moved in the way of someone who was intoxicated.

Chapter 2

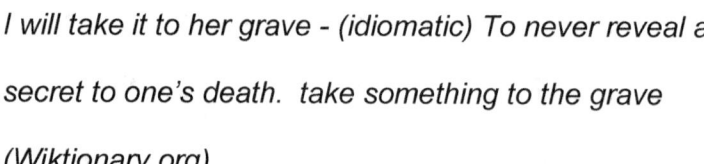

I will take it to her grave - (idiomatic) To never reveal a secret to one's death. take something to the grave (Wiktionary.org)

The morning was just about over, and the afternoon was drawing near. After walking out of Stephen's apartment, standing downstairs in the lobby I knew I had to pull myself together. My family was very well known on the block and if anyone saw me in my condition, they would ask questions. Questions I did not want to answer and questions that would alarm my mother. I come from that generation where if the older adults see you cutting up, they could and would deal with you and then tell your mother and then she would deal with you as well.

So, I knew I had to shake this off just long enough to get me into my room. I had to get my mind off the pain that was happening in my body. I had to get my emotions in check. I knew I had to play the role of a normal typical silly little girl running through the block because that would have been my norm even though I was far away from what was normal. I looked out the lobby window. Now the way my block was set up is in front of all the buildings there were benches where the older ladies sat and gossiped for, they knew everybody's business and told it all. In the middle of the block, you had tables where the old men played chess/checkers and backgammon, whatever that is.

The basketball court was located right in the center of the block. That's where the young men played ball, rolled dice, blasted their music from boomboxes, smoked weed and checked out the girls walking past. In between all of that you had kids riding their bikes, rollerblading, playing double Dutch or hopscotch. I know I had a great challenge in front of me. I needed to not only avoid the old people, but my friends as well. If they saw me, they would want me to come and join them to play, and I was in no playing mood. But saying no to them would have seemed odd and led to more questions. If only there was a way that I could become invisible.

    Wiping my face with the top part of my dress I made sure it was clear of any dried tears or anything that would resemble the torment I had just endured. I told myself to smile and be happy. Okay here we go. I decided to go with the skipping kid's role that seemed normal. Running would have been too much for my body to handle and walking would have given me away or left me open for someone to ask me a question.

Skipping just seemed best. Coming out of Stephen's building I began to skip down the walkway. Passing the old ladies gossiping on the bench I said," Good morning," as I skipped on by. I was about twenty skips away from my building. I saw my friends playing jump rope. Luckily, they didn't see me because they were arguing about who's going to jump first. So typical of them. I arrived at the door to the entrance of my building.

Before I could ring the doorbell, Mr. Johnson walked out the building carrying his rolled-up newspaper in one hand and coffee in the other hand. He lived on the third floor same as me, just across the hall. He had been living in this building for over 20 years. His wife passed away 8 years ago, and his daughter is grown and moved to the South with her new husband. He does pretty good for a single old man living on his own at his age, but I still look out for him, going to the store for him from time to time.

"Good morning... good afternoon, Mr. Johnson."

He replied back, "Good morning to you too. In a hurry, are we?"

"Well, you know us kids these days, Mr. Johnson."

"Yeah, I do for sure, always seem to be in a hurry, running to the next best thing, but you know what I always say."

"Yes Mr. Johnson, I do," and I began to quote his words with him as I had always done. "You will never be able to appreciate the fullness of life if you're always running and never walking. We must stop to take in the moments that life brings, good or evil."

"You have a good day, now."

I replied, "You too."

Mr. Johnson closed the door behind me. I approached the steps, taking them one step at a time. I would typically walk all the way up, but that day I took the elevator to the third floor. There was back in the day music coming from my apartment door. I could hear "Love Come Down" by Evelyn Champagne King. I knew that could only mean one thing: My mother was in the house cleaning.

As if trying to get from Stephen's building to mine without being noticed wasn't hard enough, imagine trying to walk through a two-bedroom apartment undetected. The only thing I had going for me was the loud music blasting tunes from the '80s and early '90s as if they were trying to make a comeback. The front door opened into our living room, immediately followed by the dining set and kitchen area. Next was the bathroom, which was in the corner of the apartment and our two bedrooms located in the back, mine being on the right. But maybe, just maybe she wouldn't hear the opening and closing of the door. Maybe she would be too deep into her groove to notice my presence sneaking past.

Standing with great anguish in front of my apartment door with all the what ifs and possibilities running through my mind, I played the scenarios over and over in my mind. I took a deep breath and slowly inserted my key into the keyhole waiting for the unlocking sound as if I could even hear it over the music playing. I slowly turned the doorknob just hoping and praying she was not standing on the other side of the door dancing with the broom, supposedly sweeping the floor.

I had no plan B. If for any reason I was or would be stopped by her, I was going to be busted. Trying to hide or keep anything from my mother was like trying to run away from your own shadow. For she would always say these famous lines.

"You can't pull a fast one over on me. I know all because I have eyes in the back of my head," and her favorite one, "I wasn't born yesterday," whatever that means.

    Opening the door to the music playing, I was in a panic not wanting to come face-to-face with my mother. I lost my grip on the doorknob and the door closed. With the little bit of energy, I had left, I hastened towards my room. "Child is that you?" Her voice came from the bathroom where she was cleaning. I stopped dead in my tracks. My eyes widened and my heart stopped beating. I replied with a calm voice, "Yes ma'am, it is me." "Don't be running back and forth, in and out of this house, young lady." I forgot that was her other famous line. "Yes ma'am, I won't." Entering my bedroom and shutting the door, I lay across my bed hunched over in a ball as if I had been kicked in my vagina over 20 times. I cried and I sobbed, muting the sound of my discomfort into my pillow.

The erratic behavior in all of this did not come as a shock or surprise to me, for I know most kids would have run to their parents and told what happened to them. But this was no, "Mommy, I scraped my knees," or "Mommy, little Ray Ray keeps teasing me" situation.

Plus, on top of everything, my mother had more than enough on her plate and didn't need to worry about what some knucklehead boys had done to her daughter. And in addition to that, I knew what it looked like to see my mother become enraged. I'd seen my mother's anger spill out before and the damage it left behind.

There had been many dishes and cups replaced in my house due to my mother's anger. We even lost a good glass table because of her shattering rage. So, I'm sure this would have been on the list of things broken or people even being killed.

My mother was a fifteen year cancer survivor. Diagnosis stemming from her right breast being invaded, she then went through surgery to have the breast removed, only for it to spread to her brain and then to her kidneys. My mother who stood 4 feet 11 inches was no weakling but a mighty force, a warrior not to be played with.

That year had been the roughest for her. We were informed of her prognosis becoming worse and her entering Stage four. My mother was dying and there was nothing more we could do. For the doctors had done everything in their power they could do. There was no more chemo treatment to give to help the situation. "All we can do is keep the faith and pray," my mother would always say.

I managed to somehow cry myself to sleep. I was awakened by my mother's voice telling me it was time for dinner. Despite not being hungry, rejecting my mother's food would have been a clear indication of something being wrong. My body was feeling so tired and sore from the fight of loss. My mother took one look at me from across the table and said, "Girl, you, okay? You look like you've been through hell. What have you and your friends been up to? I done told you about that roughhousing around y'all always be doing."

I replied, "Mom, we were just having some fun." My mother responded, "Well, make sure you soak in the tub. It doesn't make no sense why you kids like to play so rough." She looked just as tired as I did. Too tired to analyze me and to inquire about the marks on my arms.

    For the next couple of days, I was able to play sick in bed. For I should have won a Tony or even an Oscar award for my best performance in sore throats, common cold and your average stomachache. But this was no performance. My body was still so sore, and my thighs felt like they had the greatest work out. Even though my ordeal with Stephen and Michael was over I could still feel them inside of me as if they were still penetrating me. Plus, I was too afraid to face Stephen.

    After a week of feeling fatigued and depressed, my physical pain and soreness started to subside. There's not much I can say for my mental state. Overwhelmed with various emotions. I was confused, angry, even enraged like the behavior my mother exhibited. I wanted to kill both, but I also cried for

Stephen. I was just so confused, blaming myself for what had happened, for not seeing the signs, for not fighting hard enough. And not realizing Stephen was not my friend.

Leading up to the following week I haven't noticed Stephen not being in school. My mother had been placed in hospice, and I was too distracted and consumed with worry over losing her. It was a cool evening, and I was sitting next to my mother's bed. She was in her final stages.

In a private one-bedroom at the hospital, it was silent in her room. The only sounds around were the heart monitor machine beeping, the vital machine dripping one drip at a time, and the sound of nurses and doctors being paged coming from the hall. They were the only things that seemed to interrupt the quietness of the room. Doctor said Mama was in and out of consciousness. Her awareness was low, and she hadn't been very alert in those final hours. She may or may not have been able to hear me or even known that I was present.

"Mama, please don't go, you can't go. I don't know how to go on with life without you. I'm just a kid, who will take care of me? I need you."

As I held on tightly to the palms of my mother's hands, begging and pleading, I wanted to tell her the secret I'd been holding back. It had been eating me up inside that I'd even kept it from her. It was unusual for me to hold back such news. We shared everything together; my mother was an open book. She would tell me everything to prevent me from making the same mistakes as her. It was not like she could do anything about it now. I no longer had to worry about her anger and what she may break or who she may kill. I guess I was more concerned with her being disappointed and me being ashamed.

A battle had been raging inside my head, going back and forth, "tell her, don't tell her, that is your mother, tell her. What will she say, or I think of you, don't tell her? She needs to know, tell her. How can you tell her about such news at a time like this? Don't tell her. You will regret it your whole life if you don't tell her. You've been holding it inside all this time, why tell her now? Don't tell her. Do you really want to go on knowing that you held this back? Tell her. Don't tell her.

Tell her

Don't tell

Tell her

Silencing the voices in my head was the loud ongoing beeping sound of the flat line coming from the monitor machine. As the nurses and doctors began to rush into the room, one grabbed my arms from behind.

Moving me out of their way. I leaned into my mother's face and said, "Love you, Mom!"

My mother's childhood friend was standing by next to me as my mother took her last breath and made her transition. She was somewhat like a long distant aunt to me even though we didn't have a close relationship. She lived far away in the North and she had never visited the big city before, but my mom and her always kept in touch over the years by phone.

Anytime I heard my mother giggling, cackling, and carrying on, I just knew she was on the phone with her bestie. My mom often made trips to the North to visit her. She called it her girl's road trip, leaving me behind with the sitter that could have just as easily been one of the other mothers on the block. My mom had prepared her for this day and requested that she be there and just like a bestie she did; she showed up.

We journey back to the apartment after hours and hours of much crying and weeping at the hospital. News of my mom's passing must have spread because the neighbors had set up a visual memorial.

A picture frame with my mother's photo inside of it, along with cards and a poster reflecting words like I love you, thank you, you are my angel, I will miss you and rest in peace. There were also candles burning and flowers laid out on the ground in front of the entryway of the building greeted us as we approached. I shed many silent tears as we strolled on by.

Standing in front of my apartment door as I was about to insert the key into the keyhole. I was hoping, just praying that this time she would be standing there on the other side, dancing with the broom supposedly sweeping the floor, but there was no music playing from underneath the door. No oldie but goodie tunes blasting from her stereo.

I paused for a moment taking in a deep breath before opening the door. My mother's best friend asked, "Are you okay, sweetheart?"
"Yeah," I replied. The sadness choked my words and that's all I could get out. My mother's best friend said, "Would you like me to fix you something to eat?" "No, thank you," I replied, heading straight towards my room.

With all this sorrow happening, only thing I could think of was how much I needed my best friend, Stephen. But he wasn't my best friend, he was one of the violators that had hurt me deeply. I reminded myself as if I had forgotten. But there was another part of me that still believed that he was, and he is my best friend. I needed to go to him. I needed to tell him.

Walking out of my room I approached my mom's best friend. I informed her that I would be right back. I told her I was just running across the building to see my friend. even though this was absolutely crazy of me to be doing. I was not even sure what was wrong with me, but I'd just lost my mother and I didn't know who to turn to besides the person I'd always turned to and that is my best friend. I began to cry as I made my way to Stephen's apartment. I noticed the windows to his apartment were all open as if the apartment was empty, and the walls were freshly painted. The only time you see that ever happening is when someone moves out, but nevertheless I continued with my run. Passing the old ladies gossiping on the bench, I headed straight for the entrance to the door of the building. Stephen lived on the second floor, so I just took the steps. I pounded on the door as if it was an emergency, but this was an emergency. My mom had just died, and I needed to let my best friend know.

It seemed like several hours had passed as I stood knocking, banging, and kicking on the door. Why weren't they answering? It was late in the evening, pretty much night. Stephen's mom would have been home from work by now and Stephen would have had to be home as well, for it was close enough to curfew.

They weren't the type of people that went out on weekday evenings, but I stood at the door knocking. Eventually giving up I went back downstairs and outside to position myself under Stephen's window to scream his name, but before I could take in a deep breath to scream, one of the old ladies that sat on the bench stopped me. She said, "Oh honey, they are not there anymore." I replied, "I beg your pardon, what do you mean?"

She said, "That little boy that always be running behind you."

"Yes, my best friend's name is Stephen," I said to her.

"I know he lived with his mother on the second floor," she replied.

I was stuck on her choice of words, "he lived," and if that shot me, the next choice of words she used blew me out of the water. "They're gone."

Being very perplexed and confused, I asked, "What do you mean they're gone?"

"Oh honey, they moved out just a couple days ago," she said to me.

Her words cut so deep, as if my heart wasn't bleeding enough. I couldn't grasp it; I couldn't make sense of it. I burst out in tears, crying, panting, breathing heavily, gasping for air. My world was literally crashing down. My mother was dead, and my best friend was gone.

Now Breathe
Take this time to write to Our Father for He is now listening.

_____

_____

_____

_____

_____

_____

_____

_____

Psalms 92:1 –I will say of the Lord, He is my refuge and my fortress; my God; in Him will I trust.

Chapter 3

It wasn't supposed to be this way - You can use "be supposed to" to express annoyance at someone's ideas, or because something is not happening in the proper way. (Collins's dictionary en.wikipedia.org)

How can a girl who is only 15 years old be going through so much hell? My mother's dead, my best friend and his cousin raped me, my best friend moved away without telling me, and he might as well be dead.

    My mother's best friend had decided to move into my home and become my next of kin/guardian. It worked out for the both of us since I couldn't see myself living in the South and she was ready for a change anyhow and wanted to try living in the big city. It just seemed like a no-brainer that she would take over guardianship and help to raise me. She was my mother's best friend; she felt like she owed it to my mother. Not to mention I had no other relatives. My father did not play an active role in my life, and my mother was an only child, so that left no aunts or uncles. Plus, she figured this would be a walk in the park since she had raised three of her own kids, what was one more?

Recent weeks had brought on some interesting events. I'm not sure if it was the level of stress I was dealing with or the change in season, but I've been feeling quite sick. It started with me throwing up in the mornings and feeling fatigued. I assumed I was coming down with some kind of flu. Friends teased me about putting on some weight. I had noticed it myself as well, but I put it off as me just being stressed out and eating to cope with my stress. One of my friends who is older than me suggested I take a pregnancy test. Now I can't imagine why she would tell me to do such a thing because I was not like my friends who were fast or hot in the pants or active sexually like they were but unfortunately, I did have sex even though it was against my will.

While my mother's best friend was excited about being a New New Yorker living her best life, I was often alone in the house. This is when I decided to take the test my friend suggested. It is funny I did not obtain the pregnancy test from around where I live, like the corner store or the pharmacy, which would have been convenient and easy. Nope, not at all, but because I was well-known and couldn't take such an interrogation, I made sure to travel all the way to the city where I was not known.

At home in the bathroom, I made sure to read the directions on the pregnancy box thoroughly. In school we talked about sex education and pre-parenting. I have read all this in a book at school and now it seems like that book has become my reality. I'm scared and all types of thoughts are running through my mind.

Instructions: Remove the plastic cap to expose the absorbent window. Point the absorbent tip (with 5 small openings) directly into the urine stream. Take the sample for at least 7-10 seconds, to ensure that an adequate sample is collected by the testing device. I did just as the instruction stated. Oh God what if I'm pregnant?

I'm too nervous to pee. And my hands won't stop trembling as I hold the plastic cup just below my uterus.

Oh God, what if I'm pregnant?

I managed to squeeze out the little bit of urine I had in me to give. I pointed the tip directly into the urine for a 7 to 10 second count hopefully, and then I set it down face up and then sat on the side of the tub. Oh God what if I'm pregnant? What would I do? I'm just a kid, I don't have a job and I can barely take care of myself. I can't have a child because I am a child. What will my mother's best friend say? She didn't sign up for all of this, but neither did I. I'm not sure if 7 seconds has gone by or even 10 seconds, but this one thing I know for sure: I'm freaking out, and I cannot have a baby. The bathroom doorknob turns but cannot open because I have it locked. There's a knock on the bathroom door.

"Sweetheart, are you in there?" Mother's best friend asked.

In my frantic internal rant, I didn't even hear her come through the door of the apartment. "Yes ma'am, I am here." Shit, what do I do now? My mind is racing, the adrenaline is rushing through my body. "Are you okay in there?" she asked. "Yes ma'am, just about done." Stupid reply. Why did I say that?"

I look at the pregnancy box once more before tearing it into pieces and hiding the remains.

One line = not pregnant

Two lines = pregnant

Blank for not accurate

I got rid of all the evidence, pouring out the urine from the plastic cup, wrapping the plastic cup with toilet tissue and putting it down in the trash. I grabbed the stick and I glanced at it. What were the results again? I thought to myself. One line pregnant or was it two lines? "Are you okay in there?" she asked again. My mother's best friend could clearly hear the scuffling happening in the bathroom. "Yes." My yes did not bring her any comfort, but only seemed to have alerted her that there was something wrong.

"Open up the door, darling. I'm sure whatever is going on I can help," she said. "There's nothing going on, I'll be out in a minute," I said. I took the pregnancy test and hid it in my pocket and opened the bathroom door. My mother's best friend stood at the bathroom door with the receipt of the pregnancy test I had purchased and said, "I think you dropped this."

The look of shame was written all over my face. I felt so little, so stupid in that moment I could barely look into the eyes of my new guardian. A kind gentle woman who all she wanted to do was just help her best friend's child. I felt like I had betrayed her or even swindled her into this misconception of life I was living.

"Is there something you want to tell me?" The words of her voice were firm and yet full of concern.

Immediately, huge globs of tears streamed down the sides of my face. I am silent, there are no words to be spoken. I thought to myself, I'm not the sweet, trustworthy, responsible child my mother once told her about all these years. I'm not sure what was running through her head nor mine.

"I need you to tell me what's going on." I stood there in silence, frozen in front of her. Just as a deer is stuck paralyzed with fear, staring into the headlights of an oncoming car heading full force right toward them.

"Child today," with a little bit more aggression in her voice.

"I... I... I don't know how to read the results."

"Well," she said, "it depends on what kind of test you purchased." She gave me a rundown of several types of pregnancy tests available to take. And then she asked me the question,

"Are you pregnant?"

With great hesitation and shakiness in my voice I replied, "I don't know."

"Well, didn't you read the box instructions?" she asked.

"Yes ma'am, I did, and I forgot, but there are these lines."

"Okay, and how many did you get, one or two?" she asked.

I fumbled through my pocket to pull out the tube, which held the results. Holding the tube in my hands I looked down at it and said, "Two, it has two lines."

"So, you're pregnant."

"I'm pregnant?!"

Chapter 4

I did not sign up for this - The idea of when life throws you a curve ball unexpected, not planned or prepared for.

"I don't know what I'm going to do," I cried out.

Sitting in the school counselor's office,

"Keva, you have options," Miss Winfield said.

She has been my counselor since my freshman year of high school. She has been the only one I was ever able to talk to and tell what's been going on totally openly and honestly.

"Does she know? Did you tell her?" Miss Winfield asked as she referred to my horrific encounter a few months ago. I responded, "No, I couldn't bring myself to say it. I don't know if she would have believed me anyhow; I don't know if anybody will believe me. I can barely believe it myself. He was my best friend, my best friend. I was raped by my best friend." The words came out of my mouth with both sadness and anger. I haven't said it out loud or confessed it often, so it was quite harsh when I spoke it.

Miss Winfield handed me some tissue and wrapped her arms around me and said,

"Honey, I think it would have been best if you would have shared this with your guardian. I know it would have been extremely difficult sharing such information with someone you barely know."

"Miss Winfield, I know you're right. I can imagine what was running through her mind. She must've thought I was some fast little promiscuous girl just out there running the streets. But it's too late now; she already packed her bags and went back home. I guess the idea of raising another child and then finding out that child is having a child was just too much for her to bear."

"Yes, it can be overwhelming, but you left her in the dark, and you left her with her own assumptions. Sharing what happened to you would have informed her of who you were and maybe she would have stayed knowing the truth and been more willing to help you. So, update me, where are we now?"

With school being out, it'd been over 2 months since I'd seen Miss Winfield, and a lot had taken place. She was kind enough to give me her phone number so I could keep in touch with her over the course of the summer break if I needed to talk, but I made no effort to call. I was too caught up in all the chaotic Ness happening in my world. The last time I had seen her we left off with my mom's passing and my so-called best friend sexually assaulting me.

My mom's best friend had moved back home, I had moved into an orphanage or what they call a residential facility for young women in crisis. I was not really showing pregnancy features yet, but the doctor said I was in my first trimester, which is quite critical to the well-being of the baby. When he said something critical, he couldn't have been more accurate. Miss Winfield reiterated her proposal to me.

"Keva honey, you have options. You do not have to have this baby. No one would judge you for not wanting to have this baby. You are young and you have your whole life ahead of you. Or you can have this baby and give it up for adoption to a loving couple who cannot have children of their own and would love to have a child. There is no shame in any of the options. You can have this child and yes, it would be hard, very difficult on some occasions, but you and this baby will learn and grow together."

I listened to my school counselor's words as we sat on the couch, her arms wrapped around me as if I were her very own daughter facing diversity. My face was smashed into her bosom as if she were my very own mother facing the glass window looking upon the cars passing by heading down the road. I couldn't help but wonder the road my life was heading down.

Back at the residential facility my case manager met with me. Her name is Rachel. She's been keeping tabs on my progress at the facility and schoolwork. Even though I'm pregnant I'm still required to go to school and complete all my assignments on time and keep my grade point average up. But this meeting was not about school nor grades nor if I'm making friends at the facility. It was about the decision that I needed to make. Am I'm having this baby or well I be getting an abortion? I am still in my early first trimester stage and having this baby or not having this baby is on the discussion table.

Rachel " Keva how's everything been going how have you been feeling?"

"I've been managing, doing okay. I haven't quite gotten over the heartburn, nausea and frequent urination just yet."

I know why we are meeting today and honestly at the talking to my school counselor I've decided to go through with the abortion."

"Are you sure?"

Well yes, I feel like my life has been difficult enough so far this year why add anything else. I feel like bringing a child into this world will only complicate things even more and now I will not only be complicating my own life but the life of someone else.

It just doesn't seem fair. None of this seems fair. I didn't sign up for any of this.

" You are absolutely right. you did not sign up for any of this and this is far from being fair. And I want you to know you did not have to feel bad or shame about going through with this procedure"

As Rachel spoke, I began to cry. I'm so confused and angry with so many emotions. I blurted out in anger and frustration kicking the desk which was in front of me.

" I'm so tired of everybody telling me how to feel, why shouldn't I not be ashamed, why shouldn't I not feel guilty. I'm taking the life of someone else as if I am God. what right do I have to choose for this undeveloped child?" what if the shoe was on the other foot would I want someone to abort me? I think not and then again on the other hand how do I raise a child while being a child."

"Keva", Rachel getting out of her chair coming around from the desk where she sat. She speaks in a calm tone voice "you do not have to make this decision today. And those overwhelming and confusing"
"No, you can set up the appointment I don't want to keep going back and forth I prefer to get this over with" "I need you to be absolutely sure about this decision. You should take some more time to think about it. I can even set up the appointment for later next week. this will buy you time to make your final decision."

"Fine, just fine (in my most hormonal aggravated frustration voice) but I know I'm not going to change my mind I can't keep doing this"
The days scenes drag at times and then there's moments where the days seem to just fly right on by, especially when I was napping, and I'm sleep a lot. I

wrestle back and forth with the idea of getting rid of the baby but as the days draw closer and closer until my appointment. I struggle to stay focused in school. Imagine trying to solve for X or to find the square root of 77 man please I can't even solve or find the root of my own life let alone a number I can't remember hours leading up to my appointment. My palm was so sweaty for some reason I had butterflies in my stomach. I was sure I was determined to get this over with. For I was so finished with the sleepless nights of back pain, heart burns, non-stop trips to the bathroom and the constant reminder of what happened to me that caused me to get pregnant in the first place. I just wanted it all to be over, to crawl on a rock and pretend like none of it even happened.

The moment has come. I'm here facing the front of the doctor's office about to walk in. Rachel is here with me so I am not alone but, in my mind, I couldn't be more alone.

Rachel "Keva are you ready?

"Yes, I reply" knowing in my heart the answer was No,

I'm confused

I'm lost

can somebody please help me?

I don't know what i am doing

Rachel " Keva if you are having second thoughts is fine you do not have to go through with this"

"I said I am ready, I am fine" I tried to use my toughest voice. I'm not sure if I was trying to convince her or myself.

"Welcome to the Women Clinic for Abortion"

The front desk receptionist great to us

"You can sign in with your first, last name time and date here on the dotted lines and then you may have

a seat and wait for your name to be called shortly"
she ask and instructed

I'm not sure if it was just my heart being cold, but it was freezing in the place. I expected to see a lot more younger people of my kind (black/ African American) however there were women of all ages, race, and ethnicity there waiting to be seen. Just a few had someone by their side but most of them was alone. We all seem to share something in common even though we were all from different walks of life. Our face faces towards the ground as our head hangs low. There wasn't a sound, not even a TV playing to be heard. Just the AC blowing from the corner of the room and the next name being called out by the assistant nurse.

    I can't remember which number on the line I signed on to be called up. But before I knew it my name was being called by the same assistant nurse that called everyone else's name. It was time and there was no turning back.

Rachel stood up with me when my name was called. "Keva, would you like me to go in with you or do you prefer me to wait out here?"

Her question seems so simple but complex, complicated, difficult. I had no clue what I wanted her to do because I was clueless of what I wanted to even do.

I thought to myself repeatedly this is someone's life. I'm taking away someone's life. What about my life? This is not what I want for my life. How is this fair for this child? How is this fair for me? How would I ever be able to forgive myself? I can't raise any children. I am just a child myself.

Leaving Rachel in the waiting room I enter the room where a bed with a table of numbers of medication, needles and tools are laid out to be used.

As I wait for the doctor, I am instructed to remove my clothes in replace of pitting on a white cloth gown. I'm then greeted by a counselor who proceeded to ask me a couple questions out of standard procedure to make sure that I am not being forced against my own will and my decision is an act of my own free will.

As the clinic counselor leaves the room the performance doctor enters. she introduces herself as Doctor Madlocks and begins to go over the procedure step by step

    I tried my best to listen to her words but my heartbeat and breathing seems to be louder than she can speak. Questions that overpowered and bombarded my mind seemed to hold me captive. I didn't need anybody to judge me. I was already doing that myself.

"Keva, are you listening?" The doctors voice grabs my attention back "So, I will start with injecting a number of medications into or near your cervix. stretch the opening of your cervix with a series of dilating rods. insert a thin tube through your cervix into your uterus. use a combination of medical tools and a suction device to gently take the pregnancy tissue out of your uterus. You would then rest for one hour as being monitored how your body is reacting and that is the whole procedure."

As I begin to lean my body back against the table I crouch down to the lower end of the table. Positioning my legs into the lithotomy stirrups. I could no longer hold back the tears. The doctor assured me I was going to feel just a little bit of pressure and some pain but nothing too unbearable.

"Are you ready?" she asked with a voice of

uncertainty

I couldn't manage to muster up words, so I only shook

my head

She begins the countdown as she grabs the first

needle injecting.

I took a deep breath and I let out a loud scream.

Now Breathe

Take this time to write to Our Father, for He is now listening.

_____

_____

_____

_____

_____

_____

_____

_____

Isaiah 41:10 – Do not fear for I am with you; do not be afraid, for I am your God. I will strengthen you; I will help you; I will hold on to you with My righteous right hand.

Chapter 5

It wasn't a dream but reality – the world or the state of things as they exist, as opposed to an idealistic or notional idea of them. (Online dictionary Oxford)

"Mama, mama" I am awakened by the voice of my daughter. "I'm going to be late for school. Come on, come on, today is a big day!" she screams with excitement she continues "Mama I picked out my clothes, I brushed my teeth, I made myself a bowl of cereal, and I even combed my hair and put it into two pigtails, I'm ready to go! The confidence in her voice and the pride upon her face was enough to illuminate my whole bedroom. I didn't have the heart to tell her one pigtail was standing up nor that she still had milk residue left from her bowl of cereal on top of her lip. I couldn't help but to just stare at her as she rambled on and on about today's event at school. I can't imagine what my life would have been like had I decide to go through with that abortion. I would never forget those final moments lying crouch down with my legs up wide open and terrified. When the doctor was about to insert the needle. I can remember being so confused, full of sorrow, full of hurt, anger, rage more like it. But I just couldn't go through with it. Even though this was my life I couldn't imagine taking the life of another; it just didn't sit right. Would I have wanted my mother to abort me? Absolutely not! I remember walking out the room screaming and crying as my case manager Rachel quickly ran to my side to console me with tears all over her face. The way we cry as wolves howling at the moon. It was evidence that my case manager shared my pain. I wonder if she herself was once in my position and that's why she does what she does for a living helping us youth. We gathered ourselves and walked out the Abortion Center never to speak again about such place and what could have or would have taken place.

"Mama are you listening to me" "Yes Hope I am listening" Hope was the name I gave her the day I gave birth. Leading up to my due date I never had a name. I was so afraid and nervous about what our future was going to be like. I was still in school when I gave birth and living in a shelter. Our future seemed so uncertain the only thing I had left to hold on to be my last little bit of hope and that's how she got the name Hope. "All right all right Ms. Busybody first let's do our morning prayer talk with God" I had made morning talk with God our everyday routine since she was a baby, it was a tradition my mom passed down to me from her mother's mother. We positioned ourselves at the foot of the bed kneeling with our hands joined together.

"Mama I go first I already know what I want to talk to God about." Without my consent my daughter takes off in prayer as if I had a choice of letting her go second. "Good morning God, today is the Fathers Daughters dance recital at school......

Listening to Hope pray I can clearly see where this was about to go. She has been inquiring about who her father is for some time now and I have been reluctant to share with her the horrifying events that took place that caused her to be here alive, plus I honestly didn't even know which one could have been her father. She looks so much like me. I guess it was by the grace of God I don't see them in her.

...... I am grateful to have brother James (one of the youth leaders at the local church we have been attending to for a year now) to escort me to the dance however I would give anything to know who my father is and was wondering if you can find him for me in Jesus' name amen, mama it's your turn now"

Good morning Heavenly Father.......
In the mix of my prayer, I reflect on all I've been through and how I managed to make it here. I know it was only by the grace of God I'm still alive. If it was anyone else placed in my shoes and had to go through being raped, losing a mother, being placed in an orphanage, and having a baby they would have lost their mind. I know if it wasn't for God whose hands were upon my life, even though I didn't see Him or feel Him at times my life could have taken a different toll. I could have turned to drugs, or I could have become promiscuous longing for love in many wrong places, I could have been living on the street homeless, but God sent these people in my life. They

may have been strangers to me, but they were angels sent by God. I was able to graduate school, I never went out homeless in the streets, I never missed a meal, I didn't turn to drugs, and I am still in my right mind. Giving birth to my daughter and finding a job to support us could have only been God.

...... please allow Hope to have a wonderful time at the dance today and give her peace in Jesus' name, Amen."

"Mama please" stopping Hope in her tracks

"Little girl do not start with me this morning we've been through this"

"Yes, I know but it's not fair how come we can't at least try to find him? All the other kids will have their father at the dance. Maybe he's looking for us and just don't know where to find us"

HOPE

"It's complicated it's not that easy"

Looking at the disappointment in my daughter's eyes, how do I explain complicated things to a thirteen-year-old? How do I begin to explain her existence and how she came about? How do you tell your daughter she is the product of a young girl who was raped? I haven't figured it out yet, so I never told her.

    The honk coming from the school bus my daughter takes every morning was my saving grace. My exit out of this conversation I dread to have.

"Have a wonderful day sweetheart" I hug my daughter with a sigh of relief.

"Mama you have a great day too don't forget we have youth service tonight at church as well." Giving up the battle of the conversation she runs off to the school bus. I may have won this battle this time but there is coming a day I know I will lose, and I will have to give her the answer she deserves to know.

Keep Me Oh Lord
By Keva Pryce

For when my heart is weary, and my faith is gone

For when I am worried, and tears start to fall

Down my face like a river fall

Sometimes it is hard, and I feel I can't go on

For when days have me down and nights have me up

Sobbing, carrying on

For when I feel like all hope is gone

Prove me wrong so I can go on

For when darkness covers my world and clouds become gray. Show me light and bright sunny days

For when I am weak, burdened down with pain

Give me strength so I can praise thy name

Guide me in thy path so I won't stray away

Help me through thy days so I can say thanks for another day. Keep me oh Lord and let this be my prayer in Jesus' name, Amen!

Chapter 6

The voice of God - When God speaks, He is not limited to only a pastor. He uses a variety of avenues and vessels all to get your attention.

Healing - the process of making or becoming sound or healthy again. (Online Dictionary)

"Good evening sister Keva, hey Hope, honest Keva girl let me tell you last week your dance made my soul happy. I mean the anointing is just all over you, I love to see you worship in dance". "Thank you, sister Patricia." Entering the church building. "Will you be dancing this evening?" No ma'am I'm just here to support the youth they will be dancing tonight. Taking my usual seat as I often do. I found comfort sitting in this spot not to close in the front but not too far in the back. Positioning myself to get a good view of Hope as she dances. All the girls look so beautiful dressed in their garments with their outwardly expression just so eager to go forward in dance. My Hope has a solo, she had worked hard on it for weeks but would not show me because she wanted me to be surprised. I don't know if it was me watching these young princesses dance with such conviction and boldness but somehow the words to the song *A Heart That Forgives*, by Kevin Levar had arrested my heart as if I was on trial and have been found guilty of all accounts. My heart became broken into 1000 pieces as I look on to Hope as she takes her position for her solo. Hope steps forward as the other girl stepped back. She begins with a spin, her hands upon her heart.

🎼 "I wanna heart that forgives"

Her feet placed in 5th position; she leans over with her hands still upon her chess, she bends in a downward upward motion.

🎼 "When the pain is so deep"

And it's so hard to speak about it to anyone"

I tried everything in my ability to pay attention to keep looking on but as the lyrics beat upon my heart. My eyes filled with water. My hands begin to shake. I tried to wipe the tears away before they can fall but they came down too fast for me to secretly wipe away. the lyrics begin became louder and louder

🎼 "Just like Your Son, I give up my right to hold it against them with hatred inside"

I found myself identifying to the song as If the song writer himself knew my story personally and put it in a song: 🎼 "I wanna heart that loves everybody, even my enemies"

I found myself agreeing and disagreeing with the songwriter. I wanted to forgive I wanted to love again But I can never imagine loving my enemies. When the song has ended, and the girls have concluded their dance Hope run to me and leaps into my arms and ask, "mama how did I do?" All I can do was squeeze her tightly and cry. Portraying my tears to be more than the deep hurt hitting within.
"Baby girl I'm so proud of you, and your solo was amazing."

I wasn't the only one in the place crying. Emotions was high the girl's dance has moved upon everyone. Pastor extends an invitation for those who would like to come to the front for prayer.
He gives a Mini sermon/ a speech on the power of being able to forgive. It seen like he was peeking into my life. He asks many questions which all seen to point toward me.

For example, "have you ever been hurt by someone you love? Someone close to you like a best friend? I just knew this man who knew nothing about me somehow found out about my whole life story.

He says," forgiveness is never an easy thing especially when you have been hurt so deeply but it is necessary". Then he quoted from The Bible " Matthew 6:15 But if you do not forgive others their sins, your Father will not forgive your sins."

As people started to get out of their seats and make their way to the front. I know good and well that I should be going up there too. I wanted to be free and healed from the past. I wanted the heart they spoke about that forgives. But how? How can I stop hurting? How can I erase the past? There was so much hurt and the pain I cannot explain. None of it makes sense and I just couldn't see for myself. I felt going to the front would only expose me. opening questions that Hope may ask me and I just wasn't ready for it.

After prayer pastor conclude the service with a reminder of the church annual conference retreat. He says, "this year theme for our conference will be healing " He continued "it's time for the people of God to truly be healed and set free."

This year location we will be in, North Carolina and we will be joined by other ministries from other churches as well.

Hope being overwhelmed with joy hearing the news. "Mama Did you hear that There's going to be all different kinds of classes for dance, flags, mime, and more. Shh! Hope pastor's speaking, tugging on me she asks, "can we go please can we, can we?" Shh! Hope pastor is speaking.

"But everybody's going to be there even new sisters and brothers we haven't met yet."

Shh! pastor is speaking "But mama" Shh! Don't you but mama me, on top of everything you know I must work. Hope being sassy as I am myself reminds me quickly "But you always have to work." She quietly speaks underneath her breath." She was not wrong. I had placed work as a top priority, to provide a roof over her head and everything she would need that she would go lacking. I knew firsthand and remember very well the struggle I had to endure. I never wanted her to have to face them.

Pastor finishes off with " I would love to see you all there, Amen!"

"Amen!"

Hope "Amen, but mama."

"Not right now Hope."

Upon my attempt to leave the sanctuary my dance sisters approached me. They had the same excitement in their eyes as Hope did. I immediately rolled my eyes at them because I already knew what it was about to be.

Sister Diana start off " girrrl."

She saved and loves the Lord, but still a hot mess! She continues,

"The conference will be joined this year with other churches!"

Sister Nicole " Yes girl that's what he said" With the biggest grin on our face.

Sister Diana " you know what that means," laughing while biting at the lower side of her lip.

And before I can even intervene to give my response of saying no, I do not know she replies,

"Girl there are going to be men there, all kinds of men there! Saved men, single men, tall men, strong men, all shades of men, men, men, men!"

Sister Nicole and I looked at each other and then at her. We burst out laughing.

Sister Nicole, " woman of God is that all you think about?" Men and getting a man? It's supposed to be a conference a place where you connect on a deep level with God, gain insight and knowledge. "

My response "you're absolutely right Nicole! And like I told Hope I have to work." Diana and Nicole rolled their eyes at me. "You always have to work." Sister Diana, "girl bye you're not pulling that one on us this year. Plus, it's about time we get Hope a father." "Hope don't need a father, I am more than enough!" Sister Diana, " You're absolutely right don't get me wrong you're doing your thing and you're doing a damn good job, but every girl needs a father well hell I can use a father or a daddy myself." Laughing at herself Nicole "Diana you need more of Jesus." "Well, if I do go, which I am not, that wouldn't be my reason for going. Like Nicole said, "The conference is a place of connecting or in your case reconnecting with God."

Calling Hope from across the room "come on time to go." Sister Diana, "Wait! Girl you know I'm just messing around with you, just think about it before you say no.

Nicole, "You should pray on it."

Okay I will love you both later. Nicole and Diana "See you later Hope." Hope grabbing my hand we begin to head out. Pastor still stood at the doors of the sanctuary as if he was waiting for me. Unlike everyone else who's just hugging him and leaving I can see my hug was going to turn into a conversation. "Great word on tonight pastor."

Pastor "Thank you sister Keva, will we be seeing you this year at the conference?" Here we go I just knew it. "No pastor, I have to work. "Hope chimes in "she always has to work." Me squeezing her hand tightly to indicate that she should be quiet. Pastor "You know Sister Keva your job will always be there, but a conference comes and go they're never the same and I'm expecting great things from this conference, greater than the last."

"That is awesome and if I could get out of work I would…" stopping me in my tracks,

Pastor, " Sister Keva you remind me of my daughter. cheerful, pleasant, hardworking, always wearing a smile and having a great heart, however it is that same heart that carries all the hurt, pain, and anger. Even though you do not speak it to anyone, a good father can always see and tell when his children are hurting." "Pastor I am fine, yes it has been a rough year of course but I've come through a lot."

Pastor, "And that's what the conference is focused on this year. Healing from the past hurts. God's Ultimate Healing Power. All I ask is that you pray and truly seek God for direction, Amen!"

"Amen Pastor, see you next week."

Now Breathe
Take this time to write to Our Father, for He is now listening.

_____

_____

_____

_____

_____

_____

_____

John 14:27 – Peace I leave with you, my peace I give unto you: not as the world giveth, give I unto you. Let not your heart be troubled, neither let it be afraid.

Chapter 7

Arrest to seize (someone) by legal authority and take into custody (online Dictionary)

Spiritual arrest

"There's a point in our relationship with God and our walk with Christ where we must allow the Holy Spirit to place us Under Spiritual Arrest. It's not a pleasant feeling, but one that I believe is mandatory if one is going to execute and fulfill the [their] divine destiny" - Rev. Mark J. Lyons

Being awakened by the concern and voice of my daughter. "Mama, mama wake up you're making those weird noises again. As if you were screaming but not screaming or talking but not talking. I can hear them all the way from my bedroom. Plus, if you don't get up, I'm going to be late for school and you're going to be late for work. Why do you make noise when you are sleeping? What are you dreaming about? Are you having a nightmare?"

I often have nightmares of that horrible day at Stephen house. Sometimes the dreams just seem so realistic. The holding down of my hands and pulling down of my underwear as if it's really happening again. I'm unaware that I am only dreaming, and I had no idea that the screaming in my dreams was a scream my child could hear down the hall. " No Hope I'm not having a nightmare; did you get yourself ready for school?"

"Yes, ma'am I did. But mama, are you sure you're not having a nightmare because from the sounds of it…."

"No Hope I am fine! let's do our morning prayer talk with God"

We positioned ourselves at the foot of the bed kneeling with our hands joined together.

With the biggest smile on her face Hope said, "Mama can I go first I already know what I want to talk to God about." With a big grin on my face, I replied, "I am sure you do! Go head Hope."

"Good morning God...."

I typically would zone out as Hope begins to pray. it's not by choice nor is her prayer not important to me. But home girl does tend to be a little long winded but, on this morning, she seemed to grasp my attention

".... the conference trip is weeks ahead and it would mean the world to me to go plus all my friends from dance are going. Can you help my mom to see if not for me then for herself? In Jesus name:

Hope "Amen."

Mom "Amen."

Sweetheart what did you mean in your prayer if not for me then for her?"

(School bus honk)

Hope "I don't know mom I just really really want to go can't you understand? I have to go,"

Have a wonderful day at school.

Hope "have a great day at work."

One thing I can say about my child is that she's smart and she was about to be right. If I didn't start getting ready and heading out the door, I was going to be late for work.

Jumping into the car

Seat belt on

I start the engine

The radio comes on

I put the car in reverse

Looking into my rearview mirror to start heading backwards. It was as if I had been arrested. I stopped suddenly in my tracks.

♪ *"I want a heart that forgives*

A heart full of love."

Coming from the car radio

♪ *"One with compassion just like Yours above."*

Once again tears rushed down my face. I just cannot believe it. Shock, dumbfounded. Hope was just dancing to this song in church and now I'm hearing it in the car.

♪ *"Like it never happened, never holding a grudge"*

Putting the car back into park mode. Instantaneously begin to sob like a baby.

It was in the next stanza of words that broke me. I couldn't understand it, I didn't know what it meant to me, but it cut real deep to my core.

Wanna heart that forgives

When the ones that are closest

That I've known the longest hurt me the most

I still wanna love them just like You loved me

Even though I'm hurting

It was at this moment I blurted it out.

" God please, I don't want to hurt anymore!

Make it stop! Make it stop please,

I don't want to hurt no more,

Please! Please! Please!

Please take away the pain!

I can't take it anymore!

Screaming to the top of my lungs

I spoke to God in gibberish gasping for my next

breath as if I was running a marathon.

I will do whatever you want me to do just please take

the pain away Father please!

Chapter 8

The beginning of healing Matthew 9:22 ESV

Jesus turned, and seeing her he said, "Take heart, daughter; your faith has made you well." And instantly the woman was made well.

"I got you now;"

"Keep still bitch!"

"No, let me go!"

"Stephen! Come back, I got her! I got her!"

Ooouch!

"Shut up and take this!"

"Feel good? Yeah, it does."

"Feel real good right cuz?"

Stephen "yeses."

"Keva! Keva! Keevvva!"

Girls wake up! You're keeping more noise than the kids in the back of this bus.

I am *(Waking up on a moving bus loaded with church members and screaming kids playing)*

What's that all about anyhow you're having nightmare? Ask Sister Diana "Sounds pretty serious. You're breathing heavy and sweating bullets. How long has this been going on?"

It's nothing, how long have I been out for? You knocked out just before we started singing hymns. I don't know how you can sleep on this rocky bus and all those kids in the back, but you were out like a light. Now you sure you, ok? I know a nightmare when I see one, I have a few myself.

No, no I am good I am sure

"Well, if you want to talk about it, I'm here."

How far away from the place are we now?

Sister Nicole, "Girl you must have been tired, you done slept the whole ride. We are just about here.

As sister Nicole finishes up her sentence the bus makes a turn and pulls up to this skyscraping building with this long driveway. Beautiful lights shine upon the grand all white and gold, arch windows building. Other buses lineup to make the entrance into the parking lot to unload the tons of people it held. if I didn't know any better, I would have thought we pulled up to the president of the United States home.

Assistant Pastor Jones, "Alright everybody calm down, calm down, we have finally arrived! We thank God for safe traveling mercy. Parents there are many people here and everyone is not here for God so with that please monitor your child/children. We don't want anybody getting lost and try your best to stay with the group. Everyone please remember to wear your tags especially the children If a child should get lost the tag will let officials know where and what ministry they belong too. After grabbing your bags, we need to head straight in to get our itinerary."

Hope, "Mama, mama we are really here I can't believe it I'm so excited."

Yes, now don't you go running off somewhere without me always knowing and keep your tag on you.

Hope, "I will, I promise."

Grabbing our bags from underneath the bus to head inside.

Entering the double sliding doors, we are immediately greeted by one of the hotel hosts.

Hotel host, "Welcome to the Four Season Royal Grand Pallas of Wilmington North Carolina."

Church members:

"Thank you."

"Wow look at this place!"

"We're so happy to be here!"

This is amazing!"

"I'm so excited!"

"Ooo! Look at that!"

"Look at that huge waterfall!"

"Omg! You guys look up at the ceiling, amazing"

"Wooooow!"

"Look at the floor it's white with sparkling gold dust."

"Oh, Wow! Look at all the different vendors."

"There are so many people here Black, White, Chinese from all over."

Assistant Pastor Jones " Alright, alright everyone I know Everyone is excited, but we must get our itinerary, registration and get checked into our rooms."

Hope, "Mama I'm so excited to be here thank you thank you."

Walking with Hope to get our rooms key cards (Nicole and Diana looking at the booklet of the itinerary.)

Nicole, "Girl, There's so many Bible focus classes, workshops, and various dance classes.

Morning Glory prayer meet up, Midnight hour cry prayer meet up, Soak in his present session, this is how we war session and they even have a spiritual advisory for financial advancement classes.

Diana, "yeah girl and let's not leave out all the fine-looking men that are here too. I'm sure he's single, he's single, he may not be single, but he can be if you know what I mean ha-ha."

With the most confusing look upon her face Hope ask, "Sister Diana What does that mean?"

Keva and Nicole "nothing!"

Nicole "Sweetheart it means nothing you know sister Diane is a little crazy." Hope, laughing while taking the booklet to look at the itinerary. "Mama, they have a children's dance ministry that's about to start within an hour. Can we go?"

Still shaking my head at sister Diane. "Yes, we can go Hope and I will see you both at the adult praise dance meet up in two hours." Diana and Nicole, "okay girl, Hope enjoy your class."

Running into the elevator with Hope as the door was about to close, we bumped into another mother and her daughter.

Oh, excuse me, I'm sorry.

The lady, "No you're fine.

Hope, "Hey my name is Hope and I am 13 years old."

The girl, "I am Olivia and I am 7 years old."

The lady, " hi I am Tiffany.

Keva, "Hello I am Keva.

Elevator, "second floor.

Tiffany, "Well this is us; it was nice to meet you."

Olivia, "Hope, are you coming to the Children dance ministry?"

Hope! " Yes, I am, see you there."

Keva, "Nice meeting you too, see you later."

Elevator door closing.

Now Breathe

Take this time to write to Our Father, for He is now listening.

_____

_____

_____

_____

_____

_____

_____

_____

Psalms 139-1-2 – Lord, You have searched me and known me. You know when I sit down and when I rise. You understand my thoughts from far away.

Chapter 9

Healing in stages of one act, one step, one leap of faith at a time.

After putting our stuff in our room Hope and I quickly made our way to Children Dance Ministry where I stood with the other mother from the elevator.

"Is this your first conference?" Ask Tiffany as we both stood watching from the back of the class our daughters dancing.

Yes, matter of fact this is my first conference, my church comes, but I normally don't because of work.

Tiffany, "Oh do you work a lot?"

Keva, " Yes, so I've been told, but I decided to take a break and join my church this year."

Tiffany, "We all can use a break every now and then."

Keva, " Where are you from? Did you all have to travel far and what is the name of your church?"

Tiffany, " I attend God of a Second Chance Church right here in North Carolina, so we didn't have far to travel. My husband is one of the new Associate Pastor under the leadership of Bishop Right Senior the third, and you?"

Keva, "Oh nice, my daughter and I are from Virginia, we attend Our Father's House of Worship, where the Pastor is, Michael W. Smith and we are both in the dance ministry.

Tiffany, "Beautiful I can really see she is passionate about dancing."

Keva, "Yes your daughter as well, she is very graceful."

Slanting her head to the side looking at the girls. Tiffany. "Maybe, it is just me. but they kind of resemble each other."

Slanting my head to the side, Keva, "Yeah you are right. Well, you know what they say. There is a twin out there in the world for everyone."

The girl's running out of their finished class with us with other kids.

Hope, " Mama children's chorus is next. Can I go?

Keva, "Aw Hope I have adults praise dance and have to meet up with sister Nicole and Diana next."

Hope, "aww, all the other kids are going"

Tiffany, "oh I don't mind taking her if you don't mind. Olivia and I are going there next anyhow, and then I have bible focus with my husband, I can drop her off at your class before I go to mine."

Hope, "please mama can she please? I will be on my best behavior scout's honor."

Keva, " I guess since the other kids from church is going too, but make sure you stay with the group and Ms. Tiffany, don't be running off seeing stuff."

Hope, "Yes ma'am"

Tiffany, " I will keep my eyes on her."

Keva, "thank you oh let's swap numbers just in case anything happens you can reach me."

Tiffany, "Okay no worries, enjoy the class."

Leaving Hope with the group was a little challenging for me at first but then I became at ease once I entered my class.

Our dance instructor had soaking gospel music playing and had us stand in a circle while she opened us up in prayer.

We began with some stretching and then we went over song options. You will not believe one of the options was the song "A Heart that Forgives."

I immediately joined them that selected the song not to be picked. We're not going to discuss how that song had me in my car. We have all agreed on a song I have never heard of before, but the lyrics were beautiful. After coming up with some creative movement for the beginning of the song our session was over. We gathered back in a circle to close out in prayer as we did to open but this time the instructor begins to worship God and speaking in tongues. People from the class join in and begin to praise and worship the Father. All you could hear was

"Hallelujah!"

"Lord, I bless you."

"Thank you, Father."

"Jesus, we worship you."

"You are a good God."

"You are worthy."

"Holy are you Lord."

"Jehovah"........

People started speaking in their own language and heavenly languages.

Now everybody's in the worship.

As the people worship begins to quiet down the instructor begins to speak but this time it is in clear plain English. She walks right up to me with such a look upon her face. What was about to happen next, I have seen done to others in my church.

The instructor " I hear the word of the Lord speaking over you. He says, "I got you. What you've been through He did not allow it to kill you. There is a purpose for your life. " I even see you sitting in your car crying asking Father to take away the pain. I decree and I declare on this weekend you will not leave here the same way you came, but you will experience God's ultimate healing power."

Before her hands could even lay upon my shoulders I had dropped to the ground in an outburst of tears. I was consoled and held by my two closest sisters in Christ Nicole and Diana. They didn't know my story for I never shared it with anyone, but they held on to me and cried with me. Managing somehow to pull myself off the floor with the help of my sisters I was able to gain somewhat of my composure. It was time to go. We had been in the overflow long enough and I had to go get Hope. Nicole and Diana came along with me.

Diana, "Wow that was some word huh?"

Nicole, "Girl you, okay? You know if you ever need or want to talk, we are here."

Keva, "Yeah I know and that was a word. Like how did she know about the car melt down? Geesh, God just putting all my business out there like that"

Nicole, "That's God."

Diana, "right."

Hope, "Mama over here."

Hope was sitting at the table with Olivia and Sister Tiffany. Keva, "Sorry I am late, class ran a little over. Sister Tiffany, this is Sisters Diane and Nicole, they are my dance sisters. Ladies this is Sister Tiffany and her daughter Olivia we met in the elevator today.

Nicole and Diana "Nice to meet you."

Tiffany, "Same here and no worries I have time before class starts. How were the class ladies?"

Diana, " Let's just say God showed up and showed out."

Nicole and Keva, "She's not lying about that."

Tiffany, "Amen I hear that! The girls were amazing and had a great time at the children's chorus."

Keva, " That is great and thanks again for stepping in for me. I greatly appreciate it.

Tiffany, "No worries it was my pleasure we had to be there anyhow. Before I go to Bible focus, I would love for you ladies to meet my husband. He will be one of the guest speakers on the last day here. He's one of the new Associate Pastors. He's still in training. He has only been walking in this title for a couple of months after fighting for so long about walking into his calling for some reason.

Nicole, "That's understandable. We all try to fight with God's plans over our lives. But when He has a calling over you no matter how hard you fight He will win."

Diana, "That part."

Keva, "You any wrong sis."

Tiffany, "So true, He's coming to meet me here. He should be here in a minute.

Diana, Nicole, Keva, "Cool okay."

Standing in front of Tiffany. She tiptoes up to look over our shoulder just behind us. Turning around as she says,

Tiffany, "Oh there he is, ladies meet my husband Pastor..."

Keva, "Stephan."

Chapter 10

To everything there is a season, A time to kill, and a time to heal.

a time to break down, and a time to build up; A time to weep, and a time to laugh; a time to mourn, and a time to dance; (Ecclesiastes 3: 1-8 online bible)

Back in the double bed suite locked in the bathroom. Screaming, crying, sobbing and babbling unto the father is all you could hear coming from Stephen room.

Consistently knocking, banging on the back front door Tiffany: "Stephen come out here, talk to me please, tell me what's going on……… I am going to get Bishop!"

Olivia as she sobbing "what's wrong with daddy? Momma"

Tiffany, "Come on we have to get the bishop."

Nicole had called for Pastor Jones to come to my room.

Nicole, Diana, Pastor "Keva where are you going"

Hope, "mommy why are we packing our bags?"

Keva crying and in panic mode "Shush Hope we have to go."

Hope crying " But I don't want to go why…."

Nicole, "Keva stop just wait…"

Diana, "Talk to us honey…"

Nicole, "It has something to do with that man?

Pastor Jones "What man?"

Diana, "The lady husband? You know him from somewhere?"

Nicole, "Who is he?"

Keva, "I just need to go…!"

With all the questions being asked Pastor Jones threw out the big question "Did he hurt you?"

Dropping to the floor, "He was supposed to be my best friend...how could he..."

Pastor Jones "ladies take Hope out of the room let me speak to her in private."

Nicole and Diana, " Yes Pastor."

The bedroom door closes as Pastor Jones consoles me and begins to pray. She held me tight as a concerning mother would hold their child.

Pastor Jones "how could he do what? Keva what did he do?"

Tiffany running back into the room with Olivia and Bishop now.

You can still hear the wailing sounds coming from Stephen's bathroom.

Tiffany, "Bishop he is in here, the bathroom he locked himself inside."

Bishop knocked once on the door.

Bishop, "Stephen, Son it's me open up and let's talk about what's going on."

Tiffany, "I think it has something to do with that lady with that kid."

Bishop, "What lady with a kid?"

Tiffany, "Sister Keva and Hope was their names. Olivia crying for her father.

Bishop, "Sister Tiffany take Olivia out of the room and let me speak with him in private."

Tiffany, "Okay fine come on Olivia."

Bishop, "Son come out here and let me pray with you. I'm sure whatever it is we can work it out."

Stephen unlocked the bathroom door and stepped out. Stephen, "She was supposed to be my best friend."

Walking into the Bishop's arms crying.

Bishop, "Who was son? that lady?"

Stephen, "How could I?"

Bishop, "How could you what Son? What did you do?"

Down in the lobby Nicole holds Hope in her arms as she stands with sister Diane.

Tiffany walks over with Olivia up in her arms.

Tiffany, "What the hell is going on? I am so confused."

Diane, "Sister girl we're just as confused as you."

Nicole, "We just need to pray."

Tiffany, "Not just pray, but I want answers. Do you think they know each other? Why was she so upset?

Nicole, "Clearly they know each other and it not a happy reunion" Sister Diana standing looking at Sister Tiffany holding Olivia and Sister Nicole holding Hope. Tilting her head and arms folded Diana look at the girls Diana, "Houston we have a problem!"

Tiffany, "Huh?"

Nicole, "Girl, what you are talking about?"

Diana, "Sister Tiffany, how old is your daughter?"

Tiffany, " she is 7, why? What are you implying?

Sister Nicole, "Nothing she is not implying anything isn't that right Diane?"

Diana, "Hmm they do look very much alike."

Nicole, "Stop it, Diana."

Tiffany, "No I thought the same thing earlier and I mentioned it to Keva. Look at them."

Placing the girls' side-by-side to one another.

Hope, "What? Why are y'all staring at us?"

Nicole, Diana, Tiffany stands speechless looking at the girls.

Pastor Jones "What did he do?"

Bishop "What did you do son?"

Keva, Stephen

"He, I raped me her."

Now Breathe
Take this time to write to Our Father, for He is now listening.

_____

_____

_____

_____

_____

_____

_____

_____

Psalms 91:7 – A thousand shall fall at thy side, and ten thousand at thy right hand; but it shall not come nigh thee.

Chapter 11

Confession is not just exposure but healing- Keva Pryce

When I kept silent, my bones wasted away through my groaning all day long. (Online Bible Psalm 32:3)

    Still standing in the quietness of Stephen's room. Looks of concern and disappointment was upon the face of Bishop Right as he looked toward Stephen for clarity.

Stephen pacing the floor back-and-forth, tears still falling like waterfalls from his eyes.

" I don't know what we were thinking. I'm not sure I was even thinking at all."

"So stupid"

"For so long I tried to put it behind me. I have dreams that have tormented me that day. I wake up in a puddle of cold sweat" "I wanted to apologize. I really did! But my mom's job transferred her, and we had to move right away." "She never showed up to school that Monday and I don't blame her especially after we threatened her not to tell anybody."

Stephen, what do you mean we?

Sitting on the floor in Sister Keva's room as Pastor Jones holds Keva in her arms as a mother holding their daughter.

Keva, Sweetheart, are you sure that is the man that has violated you?"

Yes, one of them.

What do you mean by one of them?

Back in Stephen's room.

Son, tell me this is not true.

Bishop, it's true my cousin and I raped my once was best friend. I have hidden this secret for years now from my mother, father, from you, my wife. Praying somehow, I could just erase, no eliminate my past and just be the person I am now. I'm a good man! Bishop, I am a good man!

Stephen, where is your cousin now?

He died while in prison. He just couldn't seem to clean up his life. Years of petty crime and still violating women. One day, running with the wrong crowd they decided to rob a bank. They were successful at first but later got caught. He was sentenced to eight years without parole. While in prison a gang member serving a life sentence, recognized him, Michael, as the guy in the story his sister told him some years ago. His sister was the one he and his cousin raped, she described it in detail and was clear about his identy. They killed him while in the yard.

Wow! Karma sure has a way of coming back around.

Back in Keva's room.

Oh, sweetheart I'm so sorry that happened to you. Why didn't you tell us? We are your spiritual parents, not just Pastors. I have held that secret for over ten years now from my mother, my guardian, my friends, and the church...." And from Hope. Is that right?" Especially Hope." So let me guess, she is the result of that raped." I couldn't go through with abortion and adoption seem to be equally as cruel. She asked about her father, but I never had the heart to tell her. How could I? What would she think? I can't have her thinking less of herself or blaming herself for something she had no control over. I just want her to know that she's love beyond measure. Do you know which one the father is?"

No, I cannot say with certainty I never even tried to look for them.

Back in Stephen's room.

Son, yes, you are a good man with a troubling past that cannot be just erased nor eliminated and no longer hidden. It is my belief that God has not exposed you to dispose of you. For you still have purpose and even in this darkness, this mess, this unspeakable event that has taken place years ago God still seeks to get the glory and to bring healing. For in the bible James 5:16 tells us what to do when we sin against one another." Therefore, confess your sins to each other and pray for each other so that you may be healed. The prayer of a righteous person has great power as it is working. How can God truly love a person like me? How can my sins be forgiven with such a hatred act?"

You know as well as I do that God loves you so much that he sent his only begotten son, and once we have confessed and repented from our sins, he blotted them out and remembers them no more and finally His blood washes us white as well. Satan would love for us to keep this a secret and not to speak on it because keeping it a secret we'll eat us up and slowly kill us inside and keep us separated from the fold.

I don't know what to do now. It's not like I can just up and run away. My wife and daughter are worried sick about me, and they have no clue what I've done. You are right you cannot run away from this; you have run from this long enough. It's time for you to confront the past with the truth. And you won't be alone, we'll go do it together. Even I have done some stupid things in my past that I'm not pleased with and are quite embarrassing and shameful. I'm not your spiritual dad for nothing. I hold proudly with honors the title of being your Pastor, dad and leader. Just as our Heavenly Father does not abandon us neither will I abandon you. Let us try to meet all together.

What no I can't.

I know that you are scared and sure of what may take place, but we need to meet. Stay here and pray.

Where are you going?

Downstairs, I will be back.

Walking out the door, closing the room door behind him.

Back in Keva's room.

    Keva, we need to have a meeting together.

WHAT! No! Noooo! I need to get Hope and get out of here.

And what good will that do for you or Hope? This event has tormented you long enough and believe it or not you are in the right place surrounded by the people that love you. I have so many mixed emotions running through me, I am angry, I am hurt... I don't even know how I can even face him.

You are not alone; we will face him together. I want you to just stay right here. Don't run away, I'll be back. Where are you going?

Downstairs, just wait here and pray.

Walking out the door, closing the room door behind her.

Down in the lobby a meeting has formed together with family and friends from both parties. Both pastors have finally met, and everybody has been introduced to one another. Sister Tiffany is still holding on to her child, looking confused and worried. Bishop, what the heck is going on here? Clearly those two know each other and what, they were once a couple? Are they a couple now? Is my husband having a secret affair? Sister Nicole still holding on to Hope looking on with concern. Sister Diane with the look of anger in her eyes. Hell no! It's all making sense now all those nightmares outburst my sister has been having. This ain't no love affair going here sis but it damn sure about to become a showdown for a beat down.

So, are you accusing my husband of what I think you are accusing him of? As sister Tiffany's mind tries to process what all is being said about her husband. Pastor Jones and Bishop Right. With the look of uncertainty on how to even begin the conversation. Pastor Jones, everyone just calm down. There would be no fighting and there's no adultery going on here.

As Bishop stands in agreement with Pastor Jones, he highly suggests sister Tiffany to speak with her husband for there is much to talk about and to leave Olivia with him. Pastor Jones suggests that sisters Nicole and Diana do the same and to leave Hope with her. The plan was set after speaking with both individuals, we were to come together. Bishop Wright reminds us of the critical condition our friend and loved one was in and how we should refrain from having a judgment mindset and try to be more open, empathetic and compassionate. For what the individual had to say was not going to be easy to speak about nor will it be easy to receive but at the same time we must remember to find the light in every darkness.

As the ladies leave the lobby to make their way upstairs leaving both children behind as Bishop had suggested.

Pastor Jones

Yes Hope

Am I the result of a raped?

Chapter 12

But how can one forgive where there's been no repentance and how can one forget when there is still much pain?

A wise person once said forgiveness is not for the person that hurt you, but it is for you the person that was hurt to be free.

Hours have passed by, and no one has come from upstairs yet. Pastor Jones and Bishop Wright requested from the hotel manager a separate conference room where everyone can gather and meet.

In the meeting room I, Hope, sits there with my thoughts and who maybe my half little sister as Pastor Jones and Bishop Wright moves tables out the way and assemble chairs in a row. From a Bluetooth speaker Bishop Wright puts on God's music. And not just any kind but the kind when sister Nicole and other people from church would lay out on the floor with sheets or a flag covering them and there is this stillness but peace taking place.

They had set the chairs up as if we were in the sanctuary of a church back home but there was no pulpit, no choir stand, no band, no congregational people, and no children praise dancing.

The back doors of the meeting room had opened entering in was Sister Tiffany and a Man. Making their way to where the chairs was setup they sat on the side where Bishop Wright sat. Olivia immediately leaving my side to run to her mother. I wanted to look; I want to look right into his eyes, but I was too afraid. His head hung too low anyhow for me to even see. I can tell Sister Tiffany had been crying for dry tears covered her skin. They didn't hold hands, nor did they embrace each other. she just held on to Olivia with her face toward the ground. The back of the meeting room doors opens yet again. As if it was a home going service or a viewing with no dead body or casket to grieve or moan over.

Entering in the room was my mother holding on and clinging to sister Diane and Nicole. They had made their way to the front and sat on the side where Pastor Jones and I sat. Sister Nicole and Diana looked toward Sister Tiffany and the man and then looked away. Mama keep her eyes on me as she caresses the side of my face. Her eyes blood red and her hands trembled. No one spoke a word there was still tears being shed and the music fill the room.

🎼 *I want a heart that forgives*

A heart full of love

One with compassion just like Yours above

One that overcomes evil with goodness and love

Like it never happened, never holding a grudge 🎼

🎼 *Wanna heart that forgives*

When the ones that are closest

That I've known the longest hurt me the most

I still wanna love them just like You loved me

Even though I'm hurting

I wanna heart that forgives 🎼

Now Breathe

Take this time to write to Our Father, for He is now listening.

_____

_____

_____

_____

_____

_____

_____

Revelations 21:4 – And God shall wipe away all tears from their eyes; and there shall be no more death, neither sorrow, nor crying, neither shall there be any more pain; for the former tings are passed away.

Inner Reflection
By Keva Pryce

I am not what you see or appear to be known unto you

What I am is a holy nation

Leader of my brothers and sisters

Unique in all my ways

Peculiar, different in many ways

Wise and well-mannered in all the ways

Holy Ghost filled and water baptized

I am marvelous, I am a child, I am a daughter

I am a reflection of the finishing masterpiece that cannot be sold

I am anointed and appointed by Him

I am called out of darkness into His light

I am the strong foundation

I am brown dust He used to make man

I am a creation of the Most High

I am a holy temple

Not to be abused or misused

I am a living vessel

I am the rhythm in my praise

I am the root that makes me stay, stand strong

I am the determination that makes me dance

I have the faith that makes me who I am

I have the man who abides within

Who saved me from all of my sin

I am not who you see in the magazine

I am not who you see running the streets

Selling drugs and smoking weed

I am not to follow the crowd trying to be down

Showing off and acting proud

I am the shadow in my own footstep

The follower of my Savior

I am the light in the darkness

The hope in the seed

The cornerstone

The chosen believer

The spoken words in dead situations

I am because of Jesus Christ

I am the smile on blue days

I am the grace that passes your way

I am the peace in the storm

I am the joy you can count on

I am the voice you hear

I am the knock at your door

I am victorious

I am more than a conqueror

I am Jericho's trumpet

I am sanctified, set apart as holy

I am steadfast, unmovable

I am Zion's glory

I am fruitful

I am hallelujah

Lily of the valley

I am favor

I am justification, made right

In Jesus' name

I am loved

I am blessed.

Invitation

In this part of the book, I would like to invite you to accept our Lord Jesus as Savior over your life. Maybe you do not know him on a personal level, but like I said before Jesus desires and longs to have a relationship with you where you can talk to him, and he will talk to you. If you have never accepted him into your life and would like to receive him as your own personal Savior, you can simply read these verses of scripture out loud, believe them with your whole heart and just like that, you are saved.

Romans 10:9-10 (New International Version)
9 If you declare with your mouth, "Jesus is Lord," and believe in your heart that God raised him from the dead, you will be saved.

10 For it is with your heart that you believe and are justified, and it is with your mouth that you profess your faith and are saved.

Hey, my sister!

Hey, my brother! Welcome to the family of Jesus Christ.

It is very important that you grow in Christ. It is my sincere prayer that you will find a good church to call home, one that teaches sound doctrine where you can grow in the knowledge of Jesus and learn how to live for him. For the road will not be easy, but so worth it. For there is no better place to be than with Christ Jesus.

www.ingramcontent.com/pod-product-compliance
Lightning Source LLC
Chambersburg PA
CBHW071246070526
44583CB00017B/2348